SEMINOLES

By Irene Estep

Illustrated by Henry Luhrs

3936

Melmont Publishers, Inc. Chicago, Illinois

Also by Irene Estep   IROQUOIS

GOOD TIMES WITH MAPS

Library of Congress Catalog Card Number 63-7001

TABLE OF CONTENTS

GEORGIA

FLORIDA

THE PEOPLE

The name Seminole was first given to groups of Creek Indians who left their homes in what is now Georgia to move farther south. These Indians lost the war to save their land which the white men then took from them.

The word Seminole means one who separates from or leaves his tribe. Walking, or traveling by canoe, the runaway Creeks journeyed nearly three hundred miles to today's state of Florida.

There were Indians living in Florida who had been there for many years. They lived at peace with the newcomers. Later a few Negro slaves ran away from the southern plantations and found a home in Florida.

Indians and Negroes lived together, worked together, shared with each other, and married one another. And so it was that the runaway Creeks, the Negro slaves, and the Florida Indians became the Seminoles.

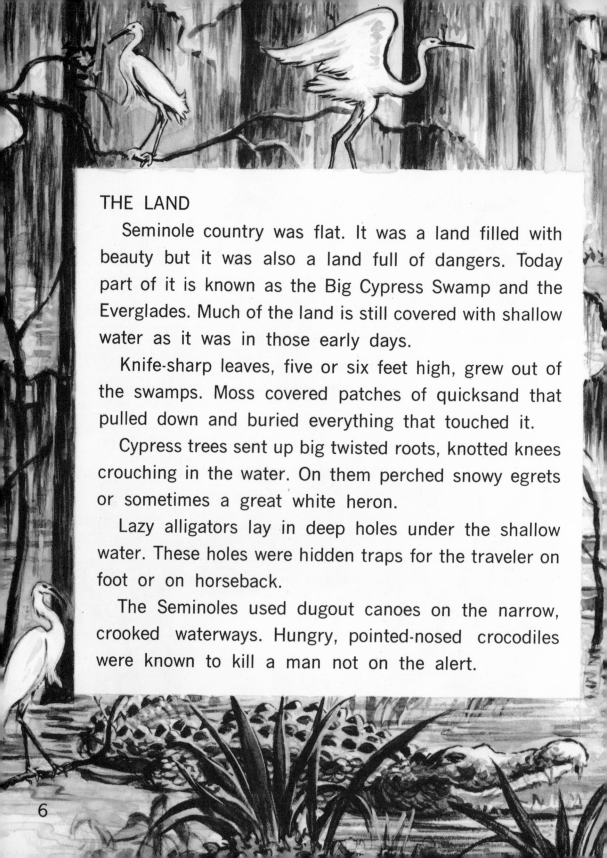

THE LAND

Seminole country was flat. It was a land filled with beauty but it was also a land full of dangers. Today part of it is known as the Big Cypress Swamp and the Everglades. Much of the land is still covered with shallow water as it was in those early days.

Knife-sharp leaves, five or six feet high, grew out of the swamps. Moss covered patches of quicksand that pulled down and buried everything that touched it.

Cypress trees sent up big twisted roots, knotted knees crouching in the water. On them perched snowy egrets or sometimes a great white heron.

Lazy alligators lay in deep holes under the shallow water. These holes were hidden traps for the traveler on foot or on horseback.

The Seminoles used dugout canoes on the narrow, crooked waterways. Hungry, pointed-nosed crocodiles were known to kill a man not on the alert.

Here and there slightly higher ground formed islands called hammocks. The hammocks were covered with shrubs, vines, and trees hung with fuzzy moss. Danger was here, too.

In the forest lurked the wildcat, the bear, and the panther. Golden bunches of bananas, pointing toward the sun, could hide big, black spiders. Scorpions might lie under rotting logs. A harmless looking stick on the ground might prove to be a deadly snake.

Wind and rain sometimes nearly blew away the flimsy houses.

The Seminoles learned to understand the law of this swampland. It was a law of watchfulness, of being ever on the lookout for hidden dangers.

A SEMINOLE VILLAGE

The Seminole Indians called their families gens. Each gen had a name as families do today. A village was made up of several gens ruled by one chief called a Miko. Each village had its own government.

The Seminoles built their villages on the higher, drier hammocks in their swampland. Near the center of each village was the Great House. This was not really one house but four low, bark-covered houses built around a square courtyard. Each of the four houses was assigned to one of the warriors who helped the Miko.

Meetings of all kinds were held in the Great House. There the people visited, danced, and held their ceremonials. Visitors and strangers were entertained in the Great House.

A round Council House stood on higher ground near one corner of the Great House. Here the Miko and his warriors met to decide what was best for their people.

One large house in each village was used as a cook house. The raised floor of the house covered only half of the building. Walls of bark were built underneath the floor to make a safe, cool room in which all the families could store food. Because of the hot, damp climate food did not keep well. Much of it had to be used soon after it was gathered.

The other half of the cook house was open. The roof was high above the ground. A fire was kept burning in the cook house during rainy weather when families could not use their own outdoor fires.

HOME LIFE

A Seminole called his house a chicksee. It had no outside or inside walls but was open on all four sides.

This is the way the house was made. Eight big logs were driven firmly into the ground. They stood in two rows opposite one another, four posts to a row. A floor was built four or five feet above the ground between the posts. It was made of long poles covered with cypress bark and palm leaves.

The roof was also made of poles covered with bark and leaves. It sloped down on each side from a center ridgepole which ran the length of the house. Heavy logs, tied together at one end, hung over the ridgepole to keep the leaves and bark from being blown away.

A ladder was kept handy for climbing up to the floor. On this floor, high above the ground, the family could keep themselves and their belongings dry when it rained or when the ground beneath was covered with water. Here they could sleep with less fear of crawling things such as scorpions and snakes.

Sometimes a Seminole woman used a square of thin cotton cloth as a small tent on the floor of the chicksee. It protected her from the buzzing mosquitoes. In the morning she dressed under it. Then she folded the little tent and tucked it up on one of the roof poles with other small things she owned.

A fire just outside the house was the center of each Seminole home. It was called a Star Fire because, to build it, several big logs were laid flat on the ground in the shape of a star.

The fire was kindled in the center where the ends of the logs formed a circle. As the logs burned they were pushed inward to keep the fire alive.

Meat was sometimes cooked on the ends of sticks held over the open fire. More often it was boiled in a big, iron kettle. Hominy, pounded into bits, was added to the meat and broth to make what the Indians called sofka.

Late in the morning the family ate one meal together. They squatted in a circle around the large iron kettle which had been lifted from the fire and set on the ground nearby.

No plates or bowls were used. Each member of the family in turn ate from the same big wooden spoon. With his fingers or hunting knife, the father took a piece of meat from the kettle. With it he ate a spoonful of the sofka then passed the spoon to the next person in the circle. For the rest of the day the kettle and the big spoon were always ready near the fire for anyone who might be hungry.

FOOD

The Seminoles gathered and ate many of the fruits and plants that grew wild in their land. Bananas, oranges, pineapples, and coconuts ripened early. There were hickory nuts to be eaten and to be made into an oil for cooking.

Almost every part of the palmetto palm was used for food. The tender new growth at the top of the tree was considered a delicacy. Molasses was made from the berries. Palmetto leaves were pounded into flour. The Indians even got salt from the burned trunk of the tree.

Cattail roots were eaten raw, were cooked, or were pounded into a flour for bread. Flour was also made from koonti roots.

The Indians cooked milkweed, pigweed, and skunk cabbage. They gathered and ate fresh watercress, peppermint, and sumac.

There were fish in the streams. The woods were full of deer, bears, wild hogs, and many birds. Some of these the Indians killed but only for food.

The Seminoles also planted gardens, working together to clear the land. They planted corn and beans, pumpkins and squashes, sweet potatoes, melons, and peanuts.

No sooner was the planting finished than crows and wild animals came to steal the seeds out of the ground. As the tender new plants appeared, they were also attacked by birds and beasts.

Gardens had to be guarded night and day. The birds and animals had to be frightened away until the young plants were strong and hardy. Every man and woman in the village chose a stick from a basket. Those drawing short sticks watched the gardens during the day. Those with long sticks were the night watchers.

One of the beliefs held by the Seminoles was that when a man died no member of his family should gather any food for three moons. That would be for about three months as we count time today. Other people in the village brought food to the mourning family.

If many men in one village died at one time or were killed in a war, their families often went hungry. There were too few families left to gather food for all those who could not do so.

THE GREEN CORN FESTIVAL

About fifteen days before the roasting ears of green corn were ready to eat, the great Miko, Chief over all the Seminoles, called his runners to him. To each he gave bundles of sticks, saying, "Leave a bundle at each village. Tell the people to take away one stick each day. When no sticks are left, they are to put out all their fires and come here for a festival of thanksgiving.

"Together we will make ourselves clean. We will weep for our dead and be thankful for our blessings. Our medicine men will light the sacred fire to start the new year. The people will carry some new fire back to their homes when the Green Corn Festival is over."

The Seminoles came to the Green Corn Festival on foot and in canoes. The people gathered in a great circle. Each person was given some bad tasting black drink from a wooden spoon. This made the people very sick. Soon they got rid of the black drink and everything they might have eaten, too. They washed in the stream. Now they felt clean inside and outside.

Any Indian who had done something wicked for which he was sorry told the Great Miko about it. Such a man was given more of the black drink and was sent into a hot, steam-filled, palm leaf tent. Here he had to stay and suffer until he felt the Great Spirit had forgiven him. Not until then could he join the great feast which marked the beginning of the new year.

The Green Corn Festival lasted from four to eight days. The people greeted old friends. Everyone joined in the games. There were running games and hiding games, guessing games and make-believe fights. Boys skipped flat stones over the water. They flew kites made from fish bladders. They shot arrows at targets to show their skill.

There was a ball game that was a favorite. It was played with a leather ball and spoon shaped sticks laced with leather. When the ball was caught it was thrown at a post in the center of the playing field.

The people were happy. They feasted and danced and sang. Then they said goodby knowing they would return in another year to celebrate another Green Corn Festival.

CHILDREN

Seminole children were taught the dangers surrounding them while they were still very young. They learned to be on the lookout for poisonous insects, deadly snakes, and the wild creatures that lurked near the village.

Seminole boys imitated the calls of the birds and used them to send messages in their play.

A twelve-year-old boy might shoulder a heavy Kentucky rifle and follow his father into the forest on a hunting trip. It was not uncommon for him to return at sunset with a deer slung across his young shoulders. He could kill a wildcat with a club. He was no coward.

By the time she was four years old a little Seminole girl could be trusted to stir the sofka in the big iron kettle over the open fire. She could pound roots and grain in a hollowed-out log. Her hands though small could work the dough for bread.

When she was not busy helping her mother, a little girl might make a doll from a bundle of rags tied around a stick and build a chicksee for it.

A Seminole child was not often punished. The worst he might expect was to have his face blackened and to be sent out of the lodge. He was not allowed to eat until the black was washed off, which might be all day.

The children's playground was the great outdoors. The boys looked for the nests of wild turkeys and dug for woodchucks. They shot arrows at fish swimming swiftly in shallow streams.

They played a kind of boxing game that required a great deal of skill. Hitting with the hands was not allowed. One player could strike the other only with the bottom of his foot while running past. Each hit scored a point.

The children played games like our hide-and-seek and leapfrog. A short rope was used for another pastime. Holding the rope by one end, the child dangled it until the other end seemed to dance back and forth on the ground.

A small round root with a stick pushed through it became a top. A quick twirl between the hands set the top spinning on a piece of stiff deerskin laid flat on the ground. Four children could keep a dozen or more of these tops going at one time.

CLOTHING

In early days the Seminoles wore little clothing. Much of the time Florida was very warm so the men needed only a breechcloth. When cold they wrapped themselves in blankets of fur. They were never without the leather belt used for carrying hunting knives and leather bags of bullets and gun powder.

During their ceremonies the men sometimes wore full skirts or a long, wide-sleeved shirt that hung from neck to knees. Soft, high-topped moccasins covered their feet. Headdresses were made of squares of wool folded cornerwise into bands about three inches wide. The bands were wound around the head until they were as much as seven inches thick. They were wide enough to shade the eyes. The folds were used as pockets.

The women wore a blouse so short that it left the body uncovered between it and a full skirt. Blouse and skirt were made by sewing together strips of bright colored cloth. Woven sashes were worn around the waist.

The women usually went barefooted. Many bright ornaments were placed in their long, black hair.

When a little girl was one year old, she was given a string of beads. Each year more strings were added until at last they covered her neck up to her ears and chin. She could barely move her head. When she became an old woman, she began to lay the beads aside, year by year, until only a single strand was left.

THEN AND NOW

There came a time when the United States government forced most of the Seminoles to move west of the Mississippi River to what was then Indian Territory. There they lived with other Indian tribes that had been sent there. This move was called the March of Tears because so many Seminoles died on the long, hard journey.

Because the Seminoles fought so fiercely to stay in their Florida homeland, the white men called them wild. The name Seminole came to mean wild, cruel people. It is no wonder the Indians grew to dislike the name.

A few Indians managed to remain in Florida. They hid deep in the Everglades. Some Seminole Indians still live in Florida. They have kept many of their old ways. They raise cattle, hunt, and fish. Some work on farms or help cut trees and clear land. Most of their children now go to government schools.

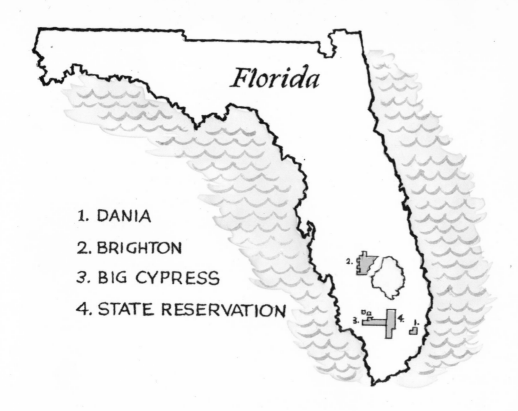

Florida

1. DANIA
2. BRIGHTON
3. BIG CYPRESS
4. STATE RESERVATION

Today, many though not all of the Seminole Indians live on land protected by the United States government. Three reservations have been set aside for their use—Dania, Brighton, and Big Cypress. There is also a state reservation next to Big Cypress and smaller camps are scattered throughout the Everglades.

The various Seminole tribes do not all speak the same language but they get together once a year for a council meeting and a ceremonial.

Irene Estep grew up on the central plains but has since lived in Utah and various parts of California. It was as a member of the Ventura County Writers Club that Mrs. Estep really began to take writing seriously. She was rewarded by having a number of poems published. In the years that followed she furnished eight newspapers in the Los Angeles area with material. It was not until she began writing for children, however, that Irene Estep found the joy and satisfaction she was looking for. She says, "Having no children of my own, I have adopted a large family of young readers who write and tell me they like my books." She has to her credit five books in the Pioneer Series published by Benefic Press in addition to two other books by Melmont.

Mrs. Estep and her husband make their home in Santa Clara County in California.

Henry Luhrs, a Californian by birth, actually has not spent too much time in his native state. His work as a free lance illustrator has taken him both to New York and Chicago.

Mr. Luhrs' illustrations have appeared in such magazines as Cosmopolitan, Colliers, and Red Book. He has also illustrated a number of children's books for the Whitman Publishing Company of Racine, Wisconsin.

Mr. Luhrs received his art training at the California Institute of Art in San Francisco, as well as the Art League and Grand Central Art School in New York. At present he and Mrs. Luhrs make their home in Laguna Beach, California.